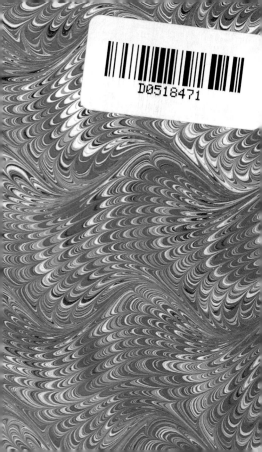

THE

Little Book

— OF —

ANGELS

In the same series

THE
Little Book
— OF —
ANGELS

Peter Lamborn Wilson

ELEMENT
Shaftesbury, Dorset ✦ Rockport, Massachusetts
Brisbane, Queensland

Published in Great Britain in 1993 by
ELEMENT BOOKS LIMITED
Longmead, Shaftesbury, Dorset

Published in the USA in 1993 by
ELEMENT, INC
42 Broadway, Rockport, MA 01966

Published in Australia in 1993 by
ELEMENT BOOKS LIMITED
for JACARANDA WILEY LIMITED
33 Park Road, Milton, Brisbane, 4064

Cover illustration:
Christ on the road to Emmaus by Stella (detail)

Designed and produced by
BRIDGEWATER BOOKS

Printed and bound in Hong Kong by Excel Graphic Arts

British Library Cataloguing in Publication data available

Library of Congress Cataloging in Publication data available

ISBN 1-85230-436-7

CONTENTS

Angels

PREFACE

his book will concern itself chiefly with the image of the *Angel as Messenger* [*angelos*, Greek for 'messenger'] – but we should begin with the realization that the Angel is, perhaps, even more, the *Message itself.* ✳

According to the Manichaeans, books might be Angels, living personifications of the Word from On High – or from elsewhere, from another reality. There exist angelic alphabets. The British magus and alchemist, John Dee, received angelic transmissions in the Enochian alphabet, and Jewish magicians used angelic letters in their amulets and Kabbalistic meditations. ✳

But angelic alphabets are not made up of mere signs, like the letters in which this text is written. They partake directly of angelic 'substance'; they constitute a system of organic links with the Unseen World – in sufi terminology, the 'language of the birds'.

In the traditional science of angelology there exists no such thing as an abstract idea. All ideas are spiritual forces, and all spiritual forces are *persons*. In the African religion of the Yoruba (which has spread all over the New World as well), the *orisha* called Eleggua or Legba presides over all borders, thresholds and beginnings. None of the other *orishas* can be summoned unless he has first been evoked, because (like Hermes) he is the 'messenger' between worlds. ✳

But Eleggua is also a Trickster, fond of rum, mischievous, and liable to transmit noise rather than information. In fact, he is *language itself* – ambiguous, two-faced, treacherous, and occult. No wonder some worshippers identify him as a manifestation of Satan, the fallen Angel, for language is a kind of 'sin', a breaking of natural boundaries – and writing is a dubious and risky kind of magic. (When Hermes invented writing, his father, Zeus, told him it was a bad idea, a device which would make communication more difficult and do great damage to memory, that human faculty which has been called 'closest to the divine'.) ✳

The current New Age craze for Angels seems to exalt a sort of greeting-card version of the Angel – warm, supportive, creative. The *dangerous* aspect of the angelic has been all but forgotten. The Catholic hierarchy has always regarded the cult of Angels with deep suspicion; the 'universal Church' has not survived for 2000 years by ignoring threats to its monopoly of spiritual power. To 'realize one's own Angel', of course, is tantamount to realizing one's own prophethood – or even (as Hindu Vedantists would say) one's own 'divinity'. To make one's body a 'Court of Angels', as the sufis recommend, is to stand before the Throne in one's own person, to be oneself the medium which is also the message.

Thus, to one who is touched by the Angel, all language and indeed all media hold the potential for a direct and immediate experience of reality itself. All media are – or should be – angelic. If media (like writing and language) have become for us a means of separating and distancing and alienating ourselves from this *direct tasting*, it is not the fault of the Angels – tricky and ambiguous as they may be. We have allowed ourselves to be cocooned in mere representation, and have missed the Presence itself. We have allowed ourselves to be wrapped in amnesia, and have forgotten how to *re-member* our true selves and our origins. ✳

The divine (the 'real') takes on human form (the angelic) in order that the human may become divine. If the rediscovery of the Angel in our era means anything at all, it must be experienced as a Call, an invitation to cross the borderland that seems to separate us from the Angel – and from ourselves. ✳

PETER LAMBORN WILSON
New York, Vernal Equinox, 1993

CHAPTER ONE
ANGELIC IMAGINATION

magine an icon as it might have existed in the mind of a Kabbalist scholar of fifteenth-century Toledo. A beam of light streams from the window onto his lectern and he looks up in reverie from his books to picture the great Tree of the Angelic World. ✳

First he recreates the bare abstract scheme of the ten Sefiroth, the ten Divine Attributes which govern and shape the universe both seen and unseen. They arrange themselves in a shape like a rose-bush on which ten measureless blossoms of light appear. ✳

Now each of the roses of light will unfold its petals and reveal a winged figure. At the crown of the Tree appears the great Metatron, he who is closest to the Divine Throne. This Angel was once the prophet Enoch 'who was not, for God had taken him up'. God set His own coronet on Enoch's head and gave him seventy-two wings and innumerable eyes. His flesh was transformed into flame, his sinews into fire, his bones into embers, and he is surrounded by storm, whirlwind, thunder and lightning. ✳

The highest of all Angels, Metatron is a prophet, ancient, bearded, inspired; yet at the same time an eternal and celestial adolescent, radiantly beautiful. Isaiah saw him 'sitting upon a throne, high and lifted up, and his train filled the temple. Above him stood the Seraphim: each one had six wings; with twain he covered his face, and with twain he covered his feet, and with twain he did fly.' (ISAIAH 6: 1–2) ✳

Angels

Around Metatron stand the Kerubim: ✳

*. . . every one had four wings. And their feet were
straight feet; and the sole of their feet was like the
sole of a calf's foot; and they sparkled like the
colour of burnished brass. And they had the hands
of a man under their wings on their four sides . . .
Their wings were joined one to another . . . As for
the likeness of their faces, they four had the face of
a man, and the face of a lion, on the right side;
and they four had the face of an ox on the left
side; they four also had the face of an eagle.*
(EZEKIEL I: 4–10)

From these creatures pour streams of fiery
sweat like rivers of lightning, and from the
drops of this are produced multitudes of
Angels.(DANIEL 7: 10). ✳

The Three Angels on the left of the Tree
are Zaphkiel, Angel of Contemplation;
Samael, Angel of Evil, and Raphael, Angel of
Healing. Samael is also called Satan, Lucifer,
the Morning Star. If surprised to see him

here, our Kabbalist recalls that Angels may possess many forms simultaneously. If Satan – in one decayed, gargantuan manifestation – occupies the frozen pit of Dante's lowest hell, he may also appear as the strangely elegant and sardonic adversary in the Book of Job who strolls about Heaven to play a game of chance with the Lord. On the Tree the Kabbalist envisions him in his original glory, blazing with jewels. ✳

As for Raphael, he is the Divine Physician and also the patron of travellers: he wears a pilgrim's hat, carries a staff and water-gourd, or perhaps a vial of healing ointment. ✳

The trunk of the Tree, beneath Metatron, displays three more figures of our Kabbalist's icon: Michael, Gabriel and Sandalphon. No words can do justice to the glory of Michael, who is patron of Israel, chief of the heavenly hosts and, like his counterpart, the Persian god Mithra, the sun in splendour. He may be pictured as a radiant winged warrior dressed in shining armour, piercing with his spear the writhing form of a serpent or dragon beneath his feet. ✳

Gabriel, who commands Spiritual Wisdom, takes the form of a beautiful youth dressed in green embroidered silk, holding to his lips a golden horn. ✳

Lastly, Sandalphon (whose name suggests the sound of approaching footsteps) is the Guardian Spirit, at once the chief and prototype of all guardian Angels. He stands at the foot of the Tree, upon the created world,

but his height extends upwards throughout all the universe, and he is taller than any other 'by a journey of five hundred years'. ✳

Plato in the *Phaedrus* implies that both the gods and the souls of men are winged. But the being who above all others must be winged is the one who is neither god nor man, but an intermediary between the two, a messenger – in Hebrew, *malakh*, in Greek, *angelos*. According to Socrates, Eros is not, as others would have it, the beautiful beloved; rather he is the Spirit who inspires the lover, who gives the lover his divine madness. Eros is neither mortal nor immortal. He is a spirit who interprets and conveys messages back and forth between men and gods. 'God does not deal directly with man; it is by means of spirits that all the intercourse and communication of gods with men, both in waking life and in sleep, is carried on.' ✳

Like the Angels of the Kabbala, Eros is a messenger, a spirit; he is winged; he is both Ancient of Days and a graceful boy. But he also plays tricks and is something of a magician. Nothing in our angelic icon prepared us for this. Can an Angel be a trickster? In order to answer, we must extend our view beyond the Holy Land and Greece, where the word 'Angel' is known, and discover whether Plato's archetype of the winged man or spirit can be found elsewhere; and if so, under what disguises. ✷

Shamanism, the universal and primordial spiritual path of all 'primitive peoples', has bequeathed to us the image of the soul in upward flight, and of the descending bird-like spirits of the Otherworld. ✷

Lame Deer, a contemporary Sioux medicine man, gives in his autobiography this description of the Four Thunderbirds, who are also winged men: ✷

. . . *There are four large, old thunderbirds. The great wakinyan of the west is the first and foremost among them. He is clothed in clouds. His body has no form, but he has huge, four-jointed wings. He has no feet, but he has claws, enormous claws. He has no head, but he has a huge beak with rows of sharp teeth. His colour is black. The second thunderbird is red. He has wings with eight joints. The third thunderbird is yellow. The fourth thunderbird is blue. This one has neither eyes nor ears.*

Thus, then, are the 'Kerubim', the 'four living creatures' of the Sioux. ✻

The shamanic spirits have passed down to the Angels their ambiguity and even amorality. The great Trickster-figures of the North American 'Indians' – Coyote, Raven – are also the culture-bearers, guardians, messengers of the Great Spirit – Angels, yes, but Angels with a wicked sense of humour. ✻

Most Westerners, when they hear the word 'Angel', think of Christianity; many assume that only Christianity and Judaism demand belief in such creatures, and that only Christian artists have depicted them, since Jewish law forbids all such representations. This is simply not so. Already we have seen Angels in classical myth and philosophy, and in shamanistic visions, and we shall also encounter them in Zoroastrianism, Hinduism, Buddhism, Taoism and Islam. ✻

Angels have played rather an ambiguous role in Christianity. St Paul bitterly attacked 'the worship of Angels which some enter into blindly, puffed up by their mere human minds' – which suggests the existence in his time of a cult of Angels. The Council of Nicaea in 325 declared belief in Angels a part of dogma, and apparently this caused an explosive renewal of the cult: in 343 the Synod Laodicaea condemned the worship of Angels as 'idolatry'. Finally in 787 the Seventh Ecumenical Synod reinstated a carefully defined and limited cult of the Archangels which took root in the Eastern Church; in the West, however, the distrust of Angels remained stronger. ✳

Christian art, however, reflects the popular love of the Angels rather than the cool distrust of the Church Fathers. Christian artists based their imagery on ancient classical art, and their beautiful winged humans are in reality thinly disguised pagan gods (Hermes, Eros, Victory, Zephyr, etc.). ✳

Basing themselves on the Old Testament and Apocrypha, artists depicted certain

Angels in the form of Wheels, which Ezekiel first described: '. . . and their appearance and their work was as it were a wheel in the middle of a wheel'. (I: 16) They move through a firmament which is the colour of a 'terrible crystal', and around a throne like sap-phire, on which sits Metatron, suffused in the radiance of the rainbow. The Wheels are often called 'Thrones', but are sometimes seen simply as the 'mounts' of the Kerubim or Seraphim. ✳

Some of this imagery, to be seen in the sculpture of Chartres Cathedral, is drawn from the *Hierarchies* of Dionysius, which gives us descriptions of the nine Orders of the Angels. The biblical accounts of the first three, Seraphim, Kerubim and Wheels or Thrones, have already been mentioned. The next three Orders - Dominions, Virtues and Powers - are described by Dionysius as wearing long albs, golden girdles and green stoles. They carry golden staves in their right hands and the seal of God in their left. The lowest Orders - Principalities, Archangels and Angels - dress in soldier's garb with golden belts and carry lance-headed javelins and hatchets. At Mount Athos, in the frescoes and inscriptions of the convent of Iviron, we discover more detail:

The *Seraphim* inflame mortals towards Divine love. They are red, and their three pairs of wings are red; their swords are red as flame. The *Kerubim*, possessors of wisdom, pour it forth in floods. They have a single pair of blue wings, and are richly garbed as Orthodox bishops. *

Above all limit are set the high *Thrones* around the Most High. They are fiery Wheels with eyes and a haloed Angel's head. The Virgin is linked to this Order: 'True Throne of God she exalts the Thrones of God'. *

The *Dominions* direct their will in accordance with the truly supreme power of the absolute Master. They have two wings, robe, mantle, shoes. In the right hand they hold a seal with a monogram of Jesus, in the left a staff surmounted by a cross. St John the Baptist is depicted as one of this Order, but barefoot and clad in skins; for he was the messenger and Angel of Jesus. ✳

Few realistic depictions, however, are able to do justice to the radiance of these creatures as experienced in personal vision. Père Lamy (1853–1931), a pious and simple French curé who regularly conversed with Angels, describes them thus: ✳

Their garments are white, but with an unearthly whiteness. I cannot describe it, because it cannot be compared to earthly whiteness; it is much softer to the eye. These bright Angels are enveloped in a light so different from ours that by comparison everything else seems dark. When you see a band of fifty you are lost in amazement. They seem clothed with golden plates, constantly moving, like so many suns. ✳

Angels

The classical/Jewish/Christian Angels, based in part on Zoroastrian models, spread in turn to Islam, which possesses a vast and sophisticated angelology. The Manichaeans adopted a mixed Islamic/Christian imagery, which in turn spread East to Hinduism, Buddhism, and even Taoism. ✱

What do all of these Angels have in common?

In both monotheistic and polytheistic traditions, Angels serve as messengers of God (or of the gods). We are dealing with inhabitants of an intermediate world, and the function of messenger is *par excellence* that of intermediary. According to the Prophet Mohammed, Angels are sent by God to earth to search out those places where individuals or groups are engaged in remembering or invoking the Deity. They listen with joy, hovering over the roofs of these humans who are fulfilling the task for which they were created: to know God, Who loves to be known. Then they fly back to the Divine

Throne and repeat what they have heard (though God already knows it better than they) and are entrusted with blessings to bestow on earth. ✳

This is what characterizes Angels in all traditions: they move between earth and heaven, like the figures seen in Jacob's vision of the ladder. St Teresa said that 'God alone suffices', which is true enough in one sense. In another sense, however, every 'appearance of God' is in fact an appearance of the Angel: and, following this interpretation, man experiences a relationship with God through a relationship with the Angel.

Virtually nothing can occur without the intervention of the Angels. Mohammed said that every raindrop that falls is accompanied by an Angel – for even a raindrop is a manifestation of being. The Angelic World is a *place* inhabited by *living creatures* – but more than that, it constitutes the very relationship between the world and God. ✳

CHAPTER TWO

ANGELIC BODY

n the Bible, the Angel of the Lord obviously possesses a spiritual nature, but it also assumes physical characteristics as a voice or a vision. To the reader of myth, to the poet, this apparent contradiction presents no problem. But over the centuries certain theologians have furiously debated the question of how something lacking a material nature can take on a shape. The medieval Jewish philosopher, Maimonides, reduced all apparitions recorded in Scripture to mere 'figurative expressions', or allegories. Other theologians insisted that the 'incorporeality' of Angels did not rule out their being created of some kind of subtle or ideal matter, so that they are bodiless but numerical. Aquinas called them 'powers' and 'immaterial spirits'. If Scripture refers to their manifestation, he maintained, we must think of it as 'a succession of contacts of power at diverse places' in time but not in location. ✳

Theologians, philosophers and mystics all have the right to define the Angel however they choose, and all such insights can be valuable. But, precisely because there are so many different definitions, it will be simpler and more profitable to begin by asking not 'What is an Angel?' but 'What does an Angel do?' Myth and Scripture more often yield stories than definitions and are more concerned with function than philosophy. ✳

Certain Angels remain forever immersed in the contemplation of divine beauty, unaware even that God created Adam. Although these are the highest Angels, they remain outside the hierarchy; they occupy no branch of the Tree. The highest Angel actually belonging to the hierarchy is called the Angel of the Lord – or sometimes simply 'the Lord'. ✳

We have already met this Angel under his Kabbalistic description and name: Metatron,

'Closest to the Throne'. Another Kabbalistic name is Phanuel, 'Divine Face'. 'My face shall go before thee', as God promises Moses in Exodus. ✳

The Eastern Church Fathers solve the problem of the Lord/Angel of the Lord in the following way. God is three Persons, and the Person or aspect of God which manifests itself, which appears on the level of creation, is neither the Father nor the Holy Spirit, but the Son. 'In the beginning was the Word', the Logos, the Christic Principle. All Old Testament appearances of the Lord/Angel of the Lord are considered by the Eastern theologians to have been partial manifestations, limited theophanies of the Logos. Jesus is the final and perfect incarnation of the Logos; He is the Living Word, the Word made flesh. ✳

If the Logos has a special Angel, however, it must surely be Gabriel. It is he who announces to Mary the descent of the spirit;

it is he who brings to Mohammed the words of the Koran. He has several forms: in his 'cosmic' manifestations to Mohammed he is awe-inspiring, his body blots out half the sky, which resounds with the rushing of his wings. In icons and late medieval paintings, however, he takes his more usual shape, that of a delicate and uncannily beautiful youth, in which he often appeared to Mohammed.

For the most part, Angels are either male – since they represent the Active Intellect in relation to the human soul seen as passive and feminine – or androgynous, since they represent perfection, completion, *coincidentia oppositorum*. But the feminine cannot be excluded from the realm of the 'Most High'. In the Kabbala, the second of the Sefiroth (or 'universal Divine principles'), *Binah* or Wisdom, is feminine. If Western monotheism has a 'goddess', then this is she. ✳

She is often called by her Greek name, Sophia, Wisdom – that which the philosophers love. In Orthodox Christianity she occupies an exalted position, related but not equivalent to that of the Virgin. The iconographers paint her as a winged Angel seated upon a throne. She is crimson, the colour of alchemical stone, or of twilight, the time which opens a crack in time, a gateway between worlds. ✳

During the Babylonian Exile the Jews were deeply influenced by Mesopotamian and Iranian angelology. This 'starry wisdom' was passed on to the Gnostic Dualists, and to Christianity. Ancient deities were transformed into Archangels. ✳

In the post-Exilic *Book of Enoch* we discover the hidden names and functions of those Archangels described so vaguely in earlier Scripture, where most of them are not given any name or individuality: ✳

Uriel, who rules the world and Tartarus
Raphael, who rules the spirits of men
Raguel, who takes vengeance on the
world of the luminaries
Michael, who is set over the best part
of mankind and over Chaos
Saraqael, who is set over the spirits
Gabriel, ruler of paradise, the serpents
and the Kerubim
Remiel, whom God set over those
who rise.

Enoch also describes a scheme of four Archangels (surrounding God's throne with their hosts): 'The first is Michael, the merciful and long-suffering; the second, who is set over all the diseases and all the wounds of the children of men, is Raphael; the third, who is set over all the powers, is Gabriel; and the fourth, who is set over the repentance unto hope of those who inherit eternal life, is named Phanuel.' *

One of the greatest Archangels, according to Apocryphal and mystical sources, was

Satan or Lucifer. In Gnostic Dualism, which sees the material creation itself as *evil*, Satan is the undisputed ruler of 'this world' – but in the non-Dualist religions like Judaism, Christianity, and Islam, there can exist no absolute principle of Evil. Certain sufis go so far as to say that Satan, like the mystics, longs to overcome his separation from God. In the end, even Satan must be 'saved'. ✳

The Hindu heavens are graced by the presence of Gandharvas (musicians), Kinnaras (part-birds), and Apsaras or celestial maidens. Like the Irish fairies (who are said to be fallen Angels not wicked enough for Hell nor good enough for Heaven), the Hindu Angels sometimes fall in love with mortals. ✳

The Islamic heaven is populated by houris and cupbearers, and blessed eternity is seen as unending love and intoxication. An angelic sensuousness pervades the very shape of the Islamic garden, which is a foreshadowing of paradise (*pardes*, Persian for 'garden'). ✳

In the Western tradition, Heaven usually

consists of seven spheres to correspond with
the seven planets. Under the influence of
Gnosticism (which sometimes spoke of 360
heavens, all evil), some cosmographers
removed the spiritual world outside
the 'heavenly' spheres. Planetary symbolism
was used with power and precision as late as
Dante. Modern man, however, is
accustomed to think of the planets as
dead shells. ✳

A few years ago when news of the moon
landings reached northern Canada, one
of the older Indians was heard to say, 'Oh,
that's nothing: my uncle went to the
moon plenty of times!' To shamanic consciousness – as to 'sacred' consciousness in
any culture – the planets are not dried husks
floating in a vacuum, but states of sacred
consciousness. ✳

The Old Testament mentions Angels of
Nations; some biblical commentators say that
there are seventy, others as many as the tribes
or even the cities of men. 'When the Most

High gave nations their homes and set the divisions of men, He fixed the borders of peoples according to the numbers of divine beings' (Qumran fragment). Like the tutelary deities of paganism, the *genii loci*, the river-gods, mountain-sprites and wood-nymphs of Ovid's *Metamorphoses*, these Angels protect their places – but in a deeper sense they *are* these places. They are the inspiration, the aesthetic shock, sensed by visionary, poet, artist, hermit or traveller. ✳

Of all the higher Archangels, Michael seems to have most often 'condescended' to play the role of an Angel of place. Not only does he rule Heaven, he also protects Israel and battles against the Angels of Israel's enemies. In Egypt he is the patron of the Nile, and his feast is celebrated on the day the river rises. In Germany the newly-converted pagans recognized Michael as the god Woden, and transformed his mountain shrines into churches of the Archangel. He is the Patron of Brittany and

Cornwall, where Mont-Saint-Michel and Michael's Mount bear witness to the Angel's taste for imposing scenery and exquisite architecture. ✳

Just as Angels permeate *place* they may also penetrate *time*. Many religions symbolize this mystery by recognizing that time is presided over by Angels, so that each day and hour and even minute has its protector – but even more, the Angels serve as living links between 'profane' time (mere duration) and 'sacred' time, or eternity-in-a-nutshell (what psychology would call the time of the 'peak experience'). ✳

Mors and Amor were twin gods in classical paganism. In later religions this paradox concerned certain mystics, who embraced Death like the beloved because it led to *the* Beloved, the personal deity. But the Angel of Death appears as a monster to most humans, even if he is nothing but another of God's messengers. Death's Angel is also the Angel of rebirth. Gabriel (in Christian tradition) and Israfil (in Islam) are depicted as cosmically huge, with wings that brush against the edges of reality. Terrifying, yes – but when Death blows the trumpet of Resurrection, graves tremble and reawakened bodies surface like mushrooms after a gentle rain. ✳

In the end, even matter must be 'raised' to the level of Spirit, since in essence it already *is* Spirit. Angels preside over the Resurrection, symbolizing the truth that Low and High are joined by an act – the blast of Gabriel's horn – performed in the In-between. Because this occurs 'at the end of Time' (or, in some traditions, in cyclic time) the Resurrection happens *outside* time – in the 'Nowever'. ✳

Contact with the Intermediate world – the world of the archetypes, or *Mundus Imaginalis* – sometimes involves a certain sexual ambiguity, an exalted erotic state often

interpreted by monotheistic puritans as 'dia-
bolic'. Actual contact with spirits is often
sexual: the shaman 'marries' his or her
guardian spirit and must cohabit with it
despite its terrifying appearance. To this day,
in Morocco, adepts of folk-sufism sometimes
marry female genies (*djinn* or *djunun*)
like 'Aisha Qandisha,
a woman with bird's
feet; these 'angels'
become the protectors
of their human
husbands. In the Bible
(Genesis) we read of
male Angels or 'sons of God' who visit Earth
to teach mankind the arts and crafts, but stay
on to marry the beautiful 'daughters of men'.
The erotic relation between human and
Angel mirrors the erotic relation between
the mystic's soul and God – as exemplified
for instance in the tale of Cupid and Psyche,
or in the famous statue of St Teresa ravished
by an Angel's fiery dart. ✳

The function of the Muses for the poet Hesiod is that of the Angels for the Israelites: to reveal the cosmogony, the story of the origins of men and gods and the world. Indeed, Origen discourses on the tradition that Angels were involved in the very beginnings of language itself: not just Scripture, but all words are 'revealed'. ✳

In primordial societies, shamans act as repositories of language, of rare, antique and special vocabularies often far more vast than those in ordinary usage. Their ecstasies are invariably preceded and accompanied by poetic recitals, and the epic and oral poetry of all peoples derives ultimately from the shaman's or hero's voyage to the Other World; or from possession, the descent of spirits into this world; or from the voices of the dead, the ancestors who have become spirits. ✳

The Celts attained what might be called, in this respect, a high shamanic civilization. The functions of bard, seer and priest were

related but highly specialized, and the techniques of ecstasy were attuned to the vast learning of bardic colleges in which the acquisition of a 'degree' could involve half a lifetime of study and preparation. The costume of the ancient Irish bard consisted largely of feathers: the poet as bird/man, the poet as Angel, or direct disciple of the Angel, Muse, White Goddess. ✳

Some might call music the Angelic art; and in the sense that it approaches 'pure' spirit, this is true. But music by itself lacks one particularly angelic function: the Logos. Thus it is in poetry, defined as rhythmic speech accompanied by music, that man reaches the language of the Angels, or as the sufis call it, the language of the birds, revealed by the djinn to Solomon. Rhythm lifts time out of the realm of the profane and transmutes it into the *Aevum*, the 'created eternity' of the Angels. ✳

When speech is added to rhythm it evokes the imagery of the Other World and

re-presents it to consciousness. This is poetry
– and by its aid the shaman, the seer, the
seeker prepares his escape from the crypt
of sleep. By its aid he locks his vision in the
treasury of memory (chief of the Muses)
whence it can be paid out to posterity. The
poem in this sense *is* the Angel, the ladder of
silver and gold by which hierophant and bard
mount the world of the Imagination. ✳

*For He hath given His Angels charge over thee, to
keep thee in all thy ways.*

PSALM 90

*I go to meet my image and my image comes to
meet me: it caresses and embraces me as if I were
returning from captivity.*

MANDAEAN LITURGY OF THE DEAD

When man opens his heart, for even an
instant, the figure he perceives (or the
intuition he receives) is his Guardian Angel.
When he hears the call to the spiritual life,
when his psychic substance is protected from

evil, when he meets certain mysterious figures in dreams, or even in waking day, who act out for him the drama of his own inner life – this is the Guardian Angel at work. ✳

If – as St Thomas Aquinas claims – each Angel is a separate species, how can we mere individuals attain such a one-to-one relationship with an Angel? One possibility is that the guardians are in fact multiple manifestations of a single 'Angel of Humanity' (Sandalphon or Gabriel). ✳

Another explanation, less metaphysical but more poetic, is that the Angel is our beloved and the very cause of our best actions – so naturally the Guardian loves us in response to our love and desire to walk beneath the Angel's wing. ✳

Angels

CHAPTER THREE

THE LADDER

Jacob, after his dream of the Angelic Ladder, 'was afraid, and said, How dreadful is this place! This is none other but the house of God, and this is the gate of heaven.' ✳

'As above, so below', says the *Emerald Tablet of Hermes Trismegistus*. And Jacob's Ladder tells us that the way down is the way up. ✳

The Ladder appears in every tradition. It is the tent-pole which the shaman climbs towards the smoke-hole of his hut: the Tree of Life. Mohammed's Ascent (*mir'aj*) is literally a ladder. In the Mithraic mysteries the initiate climbed a ladder (*klimax*) of seven rungs made of the seven planetary metals. In New Zealand, Indonesia, Melanesia, Japan and the southwest of the United States, the shaman climbs up a rainbow serpent whose seven colours represent the seven heavens. The Babylonian ziggurat was painted in these colours, and to climb it was to attain the summit of the cosmos. The Turk and Uighur shamans called their drums 'rainbows', and used them as magic mounts. Taoists in Taiwan and Yamabushi monks in Japan still perform the incredible feat of climbing barefoot a ladder built of razor-sharp swords, often as many as thirty-six. ✳

Another obvious way of going up is to fly, and this explains the universal symbolism of birds and flight. Thus, as Mircea Eliade tells us, the Altaic, Minusinsk Tatar, Teleut, Soyot and Karaga shamans dress as owls. The Yakut shaman costume displays a complete bird skeleton of iron. Often the headgear is made of feathers. The Mongol shaman wears 'wings' on his shoulders and turns into a bird as soon as he dons his costume. 'One becomes what one displays', as Eliade comments. ✳

Angels

This flight sometimes occurs in the body. St Joseph of Cupertino (1603–63) rose into space, and from the middle of the church flew like a bird onto the high altar, where he embraced the tabernacle. Sometimes, too, he was seen to fly to the altar of St Francis and of the Virgin of the Grotello. He once soared into an olive tree and remained kneeling for half an hour on a branch, which was seen to sway gently as if a bird had perched on it. ✳

I looked up at the clouds, and two men were coming there, headfirst like arrows slanting down; and as they came, they sang a sacred song and the thunder was like drumming. I will sing it for you. The song and the drumming were like this:
'Behold, a sacred voice is calling you;
All over the sky a sacred voice is calling.'

BLACK ELK SPEAKS

One need not climb a ladder or fly to get into heaven – sometimes one is 'taken up by the Angels' and visits the Other world in

spirit (or even in body). The biblical
Revelation abounds with angelic figures, as
does the Zoroastrian *Book of Arda Viraf*, the
Gnostic *Hymn of the Pearl* (which includes an
Angel 'disguised' as a letter or 'book'), and a
whole library-shelf of Christian Apocrypha
(books which imitate Scripture but are not
accepted into the Canon) such as *The
Apocalypse of Peter*, *The Apocalypse of Paul*, *The
Shepherd of Hermas*. Dante made good use of
this material. ✳

Not every journey is a journey *to* the
Angel, and not every way leads *up* in the
strict sense of the word. Some seekers travel
with the Angel, and *across* the face of an earth
transformed by symbolic insight into a
horizontal mirror image of the celestial or
vertical ascent. The sacred direction then
might be any one of the four: in
Zoroastrianism the way leads South, in Celtic
and American Indian lore West. Most
Semitic writers favour the symbolism of the
East, and in Aryan-influenced myth the

direction is sometimes North. In all these
cases the purpose is the same: as the sufis put
it, to make a 'journey to the Outer Horizons'
which will correspond to the 'journey to the
Inner Horizons'. Thus one travels with the
Angel, whose presence as guide or interpreter
permits one to find in the landscape the
'signs', the symbols, of true selfhood. ✳

One of the most charming of these
journeys with the Angel may be found in the
Old Testament Apocryphal text, The Book
of Tobit, in which the young hero and his
dog are befriended by the great 'healer' of
the Archangels, Raphael. In folk-tales and
fairy tales the youngest sibling always goes
forth to seek fortune and is helped by
mysterious animals, beggars, old crones, and
even 'inanimate' objects – all of these are
disguises for the Angel. ✳

In Islam the archetype of the heavenly
journey is the Prophet Mohammed's *mir'aj*
(literally 'ladder'), during which he visits the
rings of the cosmos in the company of

Gabriel, and rides on a strange angelic beast, a winged mule with a woman's face, called Buraq. At the end, having spoken with the Lord (or the Angel of the Lord) Himself, Mohammed returns to his room in Mecca. As he wakes to himself, he discovers that a water jug, which the Buraq knocked over with her hoof as they departed, is still pouring out upon the floor: the whole trip has taken place outside time, literally in a split second. ✳

Inspired by the *mir'aj* many Moslem mystics lived intimately with the symbolism of the celestial journey. Moreover, in the first few centuries of Islam a vast amount of ancient literature was translated into Arabic, so that the learned grew familiar with Egyptian, Mesopotamian and Chaldean mysteries, Hermetic and alchemical teachings. ✳

Neoplatonic philosophy, Jewish, Christian and Zoroastrian Scripture and Apocrypha, even Hindu, Buddhist and shamanic lore – an unprecedented mixture of cultures and faiths was tested with the touchstone of the Koran and Prophetic Traditions, and much of it was adapted and absorbed. ✳

One result of this ferment was the crystalization of a literary genre which Henry Corbin called the Visionary Recital. These short treatises or 'fictions' are couched in a symbolic and poetic style, and deal with mythic or visionary material. A number of authors, for example, composed treatments of the soul's journey to God in terms of a fable about birds seeking their king; this subject reached its pinnacle with 'Attar's famous *Conference of the Birds*. ✳

We could go on cataloguing angelic journeys forever, till it might seem that travel itself (if undertaken in the proper state of awareness) must possess the numinous quality of the *in-between*, and hence of the Angel. The Arthurian Cycle, and especially the parts of it dealing with the Holy Grail, is almost entirely made up of such 'adventures'. From China comes the delightful tale of Monkey, a great Trickster-Angel who invades the Taoist Heaven to steal the Peaches of Immortality, and who must do penance by journeying to the West as protector of the Buddhist monk, Tripitaka. ✳

We have mentioned Dante. His *magnum opus* of Hell, Purgatory, and Heaven, is the culmination of all vertical angelic journeys along the cosmic axis. First under the guidance of the poet/magus Virgil, and then of the beloved Beatrice – both of whom act for him as Angels – Dante ends with a vision of the great angelic Rose of Light around the Divine Presence. Where Mohammed was guided by Gabriel, Dante is guided by the writer he most admires, and the woman he loves. ✳

Thus Beatrice herself mirrors forth the Beatific Vision, which extinguishes all reason as in a blazing fire. Beatrice is an Angel; Beatrice reveals the Angelic World; and Beatrice is the theophanic symbol in which love and knowledge are united. ✳

CHAPTER FOUR

BECOMING AN ANGEL

ohammed learned the words and gestures of the Islamic ritual prayer by observing the Angels at worship. Ritual is what the Angels do in heaven. It is brought back by prophets who visit paradise, or it is revealed by Avatars or Angels who descend to earth. Ritual, by definition, must be Angelic because it belongs properly neither to 'this world' nor to the divine Essence beyond form, but plays an intermediary role between the two. Ritual is a Jacob's Ladder, and its celebrants climb, meeting the descending Angels halfway. ✴

In dogmatic terms a priest is always a priest, even if he is a bad man; and the Mass is always valid, even if no one present experiences the 'real Presence' as actual transformation of consciousness. But the *purpose* of the Mass is precisely that realization.

According to the late Cardinal Daniélou, 'The Mass is a sacramental participation in the liturgy of heaven, the cult officially rendered to the Trinity by the full host of the spiritual creation. The presence of the Angels at Mass introduces the Eucharist into heaven itself.' ✷

Not only are the Angels the invisible priests of the religion, they are also due a kind of worship in themselves. Despite the hesitation expressed by some theologians, certain days are set aside as Angelic Feasts, notably the great Synaxis of Michael and All Angels in Orthodoxy on 8 November, or the Feast of Uriel on 28 July, by which the Monophysite churches of Egypt and Abyssinia commemorate the revelation to Enoch of the revolutions of the celestial luminaries – though in Rome the image of Uriel in the Church in Piazza Esedra was painted over. ✷

Angels provide the model for worship; they participate in human worship; and they

are worshipped. But there is another sort of angelic rite: one in which they are specifically evoked and called down, either to give and receive messages or to enter into the body of the ritualist. ✳

In its simplest manifestation this results in the phenomenon of possession, a religious form found in cultures as far apart as Japan, Indonesia, Africa and South America. In some religions possession is the chief rite; the African scholar, Wande Abimbola, has said that the Yoruba cannot imagine a religion without possession. Whether the beings who indwell their human 'mounts' are called gods or spirits, we may certainly see them as Angels, since they come down from and return to heaven, and form the link between man's world and the realm of the high gods (or God), who never descend to earth. ✳

One mysterious feature of possession is the fact that the human soul is completely displaced by the spirit; after the trance, the person possessed can never remember what has happened or what the god has said. Voodoo priests and priestesses are never possessed; they are expert in the occult means of inducing possession, but seem to remain aloof from the actual experience (although they may become possessed before their elevation to the priesthood). The same can be said of oracles in ancient Greece, in Tibet and in Japanese Shinto: they all serve the spirits as 'horses' to be ridden, and appear to derive no direct spiritual benefit from doing so. ✳

However, this is not really the case. In the first place, possession is often part of a tribal or communal religion. The experience of direct confrontation and discourse with a spirit benefits the tribe, and thus all the individuals of the tribe. In the second place, the 'mounts' obtain great benefits from their patron spirits. These benefits may be 'worldly' – such as good health, good crops – but they also include a numinous sense of well-being which springs from the awareness of having been chosen by the Other World as a medium for its messages to mankind. In the third place, possession leads to an increased knowledge of spiritual realities. I have been told that among the Candomblé of Brazil there exist circles of high adepts who eschew all worldly benefit or magical power, and induce possession solely in order to advance spiritually through the acquisition of knowledge. ✳

In the *Corpus Hermeticum* the Angels (or planetary spirits) are called down not into living bodies but into statues; thus a truly and literally sacred art serves as the link between worshipper and deity. When the *Corpus* was rediscovered in the Renaissance, sages such as Pico della Mirandola and Giordano Bruno attempted to revive this sort of magic, in which planetary or other spirits were evoked with corresponding scents, colours, flowers, emblems, poetry, music and meditations. Various objects such as talismans were then imbued with the Angelic *virtu* and used for magical and spiritual purposes. This sort of magic was further evolved by the English magus, Dr John Dee (Elizabeth I's astrologer), who communicated with Angels through his medium, Edward Kelly. Dee devised a mysterious obsidian mirror or crystal to potentiate these seances, and learned the language of the Angels – Enochian. (An Angelic language was also written by St Pachomius, the founder of Egyptian desert monasticism, who received his *Rule* from an Angel.) ✳

Angels

*. . . and whatsoever you see of spiritual forms and
of things visible whose countenance is godly to
behold and whatsoever you see of thought,
imagination, intelligence, soul and the heart with
its Secret and whatsoever you see of Angelic aspect,
or things whereof Satan is the spirit . . .
Lo, I, the Perfect Man, am that whole, and
that whole is my theatre . . .
The sensible world is mine, and the Angel-world
is of my weaving and fashioning.*

ABDUL KARIM JILI, THE PERFECT MAN

If the cosmos is pictured as a tree, it is
possible to understand how man is more
central than the Angels, according to Jili. The
Angels occupy branches to left and right of
the trunk. They are higher than man, whose
place is at the bottom. But being at the
bottom places man on the axis, the trunk
which rises to the crown of the Tree, the
place of Metatron or the Angel called the
Spirit. The Angels are fixed in their places
—they are created with the special knowledge

of the Divine appropriate to their stations ('None of us there is, but has a known station', 'We know not save what Thou has taught us.'– Koran). ✷

But Adam, who is created in God's 'image' and is given knowledge of all the names, is capable of climbing the tree, of ascending through all the Angelic initiations and himself becoming an Angel. ✷

Angels

*By philosophy man realizes the virtual character-
istics of his race. He attains the form of humanity
and progresses on the hierarchy of beings until in
crossing the straight way (or 'bridge') and the
correct path, he becomes an Angel.*

BRETHREN OF PURITY, RISALAT AL-JAMI'AH

*Passing beyond the teaching of the Angels, the soul
goes on to the knowledge and understanding of
things, no longer merely betrothed but dwelling
with the bridegroom.*

CLEMENT OF ALEXANDRIA

For Christians, the Ascension of Christ
provides the unique symbol of this exaltation
of human nature; it is through Him that
other mortals participate in such perfection.
According to a very interesting legend, the
thrones left vacant by the fallen Angels are
reserved for the elect among men; St Francis
of Assisi is supposed to have been awarded
the throne of Lucifer himself. 'The elect will
be like the Angels in heaven' (Matt. 22: 30);
'The soul illuminated by the Word becomes

a stranger to the slumber of illusion, a "Night Watchman". It is a type of Angelic life to which He thus introduces us' (Gregory of Nazianzen). ✳

In Islam, however, not one man makes the perfect and total ascension, but all those humans who attain the state of perfection. The sufis say that every age must have its perfect man, its 'axis' – for if there lived no perfect lover (or knower) of God, the world would come to an end. The perfect man is he who repeats the Ascension of Christ or Mohammed, who realizes himself as the one who comprehends all the Divine Names, who actualizes man's central position in the cosmos. ✳

This possibility is recognized by all systems of myth and mysticism. Ancient Greece, for instance, believed that certain mortals could be taken up into heaven and made demigods. We have already mentioned Psyche; the myth of Ganymede,

Angels

the Trojan shepherd boy, also recapitulates the theme. Origen mentions that Melchisadek became an Angel, a belief shared by the gnostic sect of the Melchisadekians, who survived into the Middle Ages. St Vincent Ferrer of the Dominicans is often pictured with wings; and the widow of the sufi poet, Rumi, had a vision of him after his death 'Winged as a Seraph'. ✳

The Perfect Men, like Jacob, have 'wrestled with the Angel' and won – or rather, they have *striven for* the Angel. They have reached the Gabriel of their own inner being. In them man realizes his full potential for transcendence, and finally escapes the cosmos – only to discover that he himself is the cosmos. ✳

But transcendence, escape, cosmic grandeur are not enough. What about *immanence*, what of the *return*? According to the sufis, the 'two bows' lengths' referred to in connection with Mohammed's vision of Gabriel stand for two journeys: the journey *to* the Angel and the journey *from* the Angel, the Return. The Persian poet 'Azizi chides those who limit religion only to the transcendent: ✳

> *It is no more than two steps*
> *to the Friend's door –*
> *you have stopped*
> *at the first step.* ✳

Those who are capable of making that second step will find themselves back in the world – but a world now transformed in the light of their Angelic experience. ✳

Plato in the *Symposium* again:
This is the right way of approaching or being initiated into the mysteries of love, to begin with examples of beauty in this world, and using them as steps to ascend continually with that absolute beauty as one's aim, from one instance of physical

*beauty to two and from two to all, then from
physical beauty to moral beauty, and from moral
beauty to the beauty of knowledge, until from
knowledge of various kinds one arrives at the
supreme knowledge whose sole object is that
absolute beauty, and knows at last what absolute
beauty is.* ✱

With these words Plato takes a powerful
stand against all 'cosmic pessimism' and
dualistic asceticism. For him the beauty of
the cosmos is reflected in all beautiful things,
and the soul climbs a ladder of love to the
realization of the absolute. ✱

Nevertheless, the Platonic tradition seems
to possess a hint of dualism (more developed
in later philosophers, especially Christian
Platonists like Augustine). The physical
world, for all its importance as a symbol, and
despite its ultimate oneness with the Supreme
Principle, still remains something to be
escaped. Even in the quotation above, the
lover climbs beyond his first appreciation of

the loveliness of nature or of the beloved, and reaches the realm of pure Ideas – but does not return. ✷

For Plato the sensible world serves as an 'excitation', provoking the Intellect towards remembrance of knowledge caused in the soul by the Ideas. By transforming the Ideas into Angels, however, a greater role is given to the sensible world. To journey with the Angel means to transmute the sensible into symbols, such that to turn towards the sensible is to turn towards the Angel. ✷

This concept appears to complete the Platonic scheme by allowing a return from the contemplation of the archetypes to a contemplation of the world – a world now purified of all 'worldliness'. Above all things, the human form serves as an object of such contemplation, since man is made in God's 'image' and is thus most worthy of love. One might say from this point of view that to love a beautiful beloved is not the beginning but the end of the Angelic path – on condition that one understands who loves and who is loved. ✳

In the Christian West, with its emphasis on one single and supreme manifestation of the Divine in human form, we may miss this sense of the Angelic possibilities of human love. In the poetry of Dante and his fellow troubadours of the sect known as the 'Fedeli d'Amore', however, there appears a powerful

 echo – perhaps even influenced by sufi teaching – of this Path. For Dante,

Beatrice was indeed the witness: she was both a living woman and an Angel in heaven. In the *Vita Nuova*, he remembers how, in his youth, he saw her in the streets of Florence. Returning to his room, he fell into : ✳

a pleasant slumber, wherein a marvellous vision was presented to me: for there appeared to be in my room a mist of the colour of fire, within the which I discerned the figure of a lord of terrible aspect to such as should gaze upon him [Eros], but who seemed therewithal to rejoice inwardly that it was a marvel to see. Speaking he said many things, among the which I could understand but few; and of these, this: 'I am thy master.' In his arms it seemed to me that a person was sleeping, naked but for a blood-coloured cloth; upon whom looking very attentively, I knew that it was [Beatrice]. And he who held her held also in his hand a thing that was burning in flames; and he said to me, 'Behold thy heart.' But when he had remained with me a little while, I thought that he set himself to awaken her that slept; after the which he made her eat that thing which flamed in his hand; and she ate it as one fearing. ✴

Here we are once again in the presence of that greatest of all messengers between heaven and earth, Love himself. In a crimson flow the Archangel presides over the moment of the poet's encounter with his destiny, his love, his soul, his Angel. At the very moment of the encounter, with the eating of the flaming heart, the final consummation is foreshadowed: the union of the soul with God through the Angelic beloved. ✳